Table of Contents:

Nouns ----- Commom and Proper Nouns

Pronouns ------ Possessive pronoun

Verbs ------ Action verbs

Subject-verb agreement

Verb tense   Contractions

Articles   Capitalization

Adjectives

Prepositions

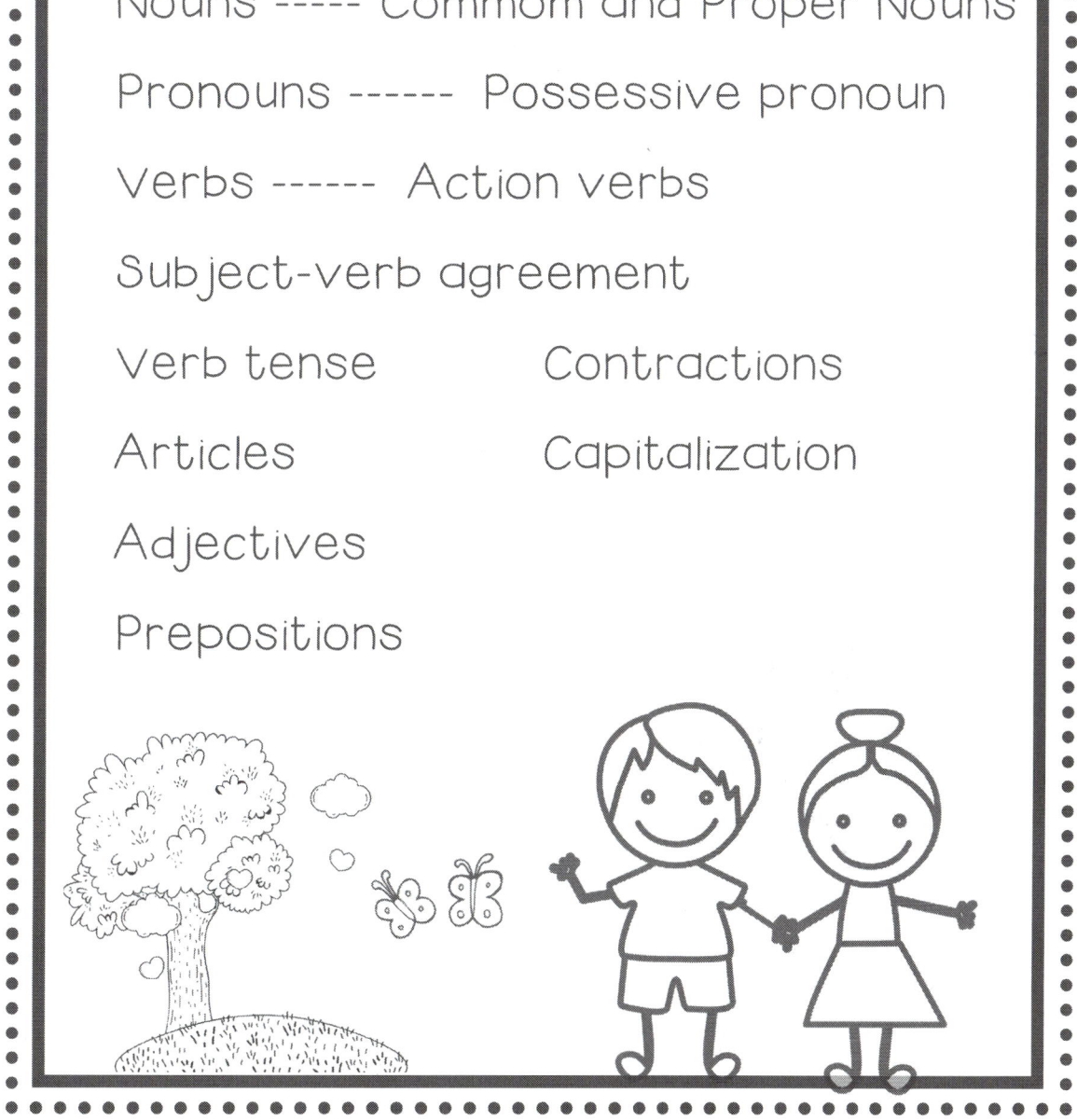

mother (controlbnovi)

Opineon is

what a peson thinks But the other peson doseind like it

GRAMMAR GAMES AND ACTIVITIES

NO.1 workbook

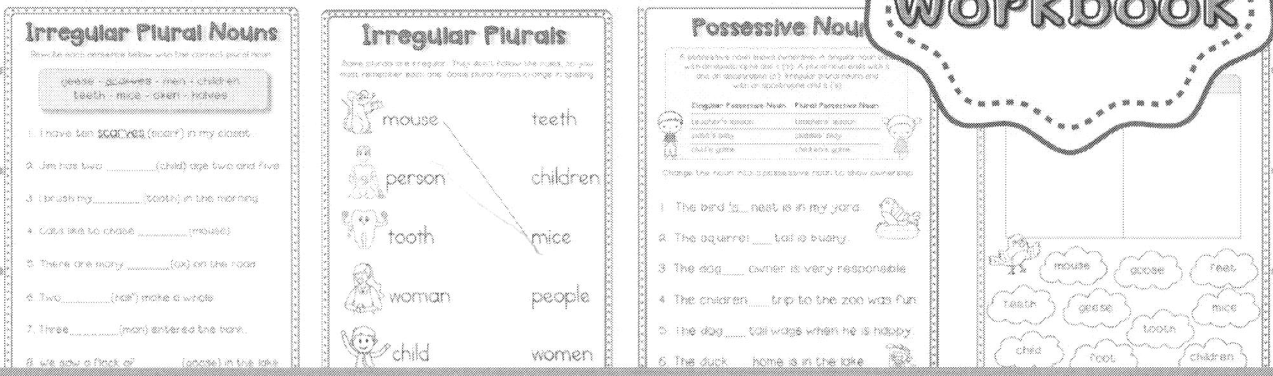

FIRST GRADE GRAMMAR KIDS WORKBOOK

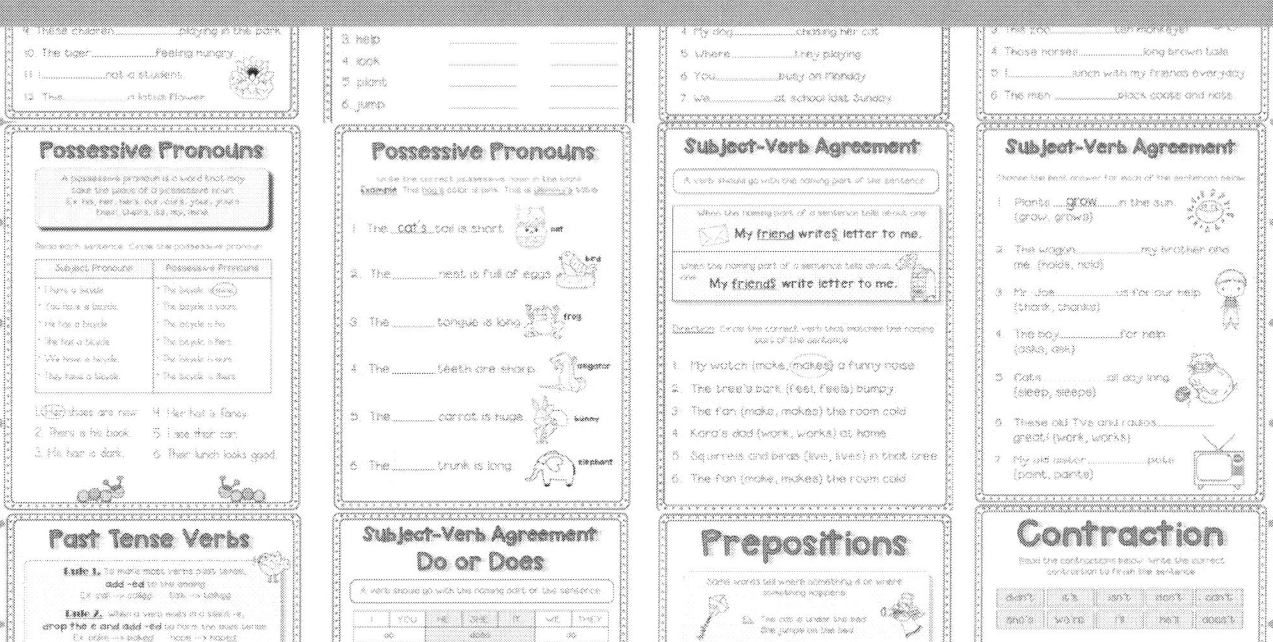

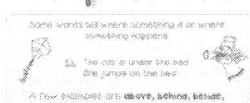

All About Nouns

All of the objects we see around us are nouns!
Nouns can be people, animals, places and things!

Person

Animal

Place

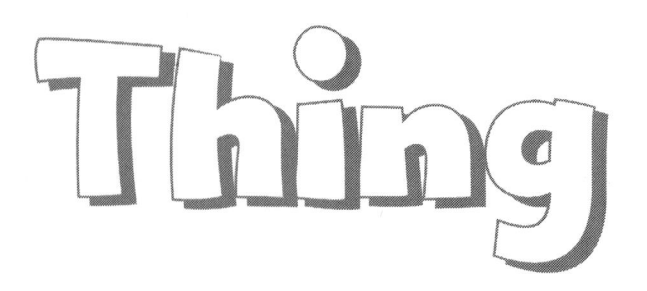

Thing

All About Nouns

All of the objects we see around us are nouns!
Nouns can be people, animals, places and things!

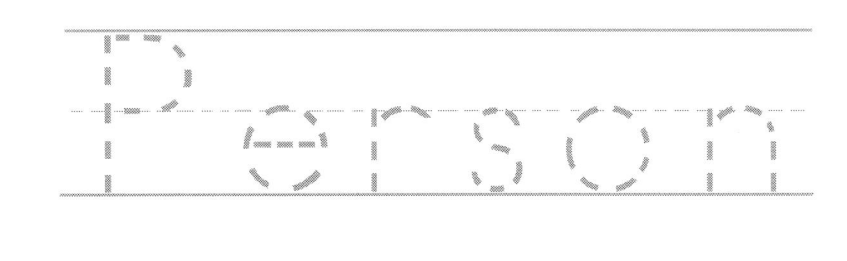

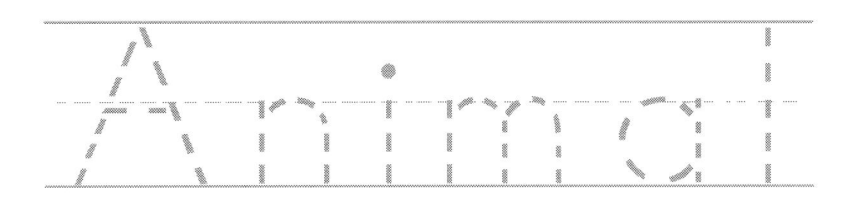

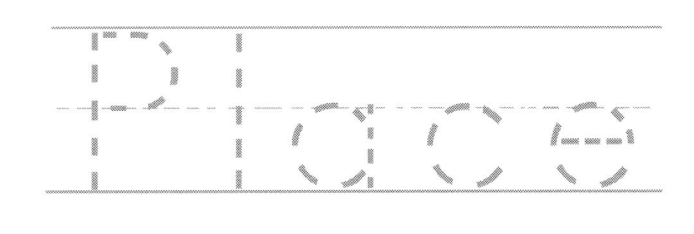

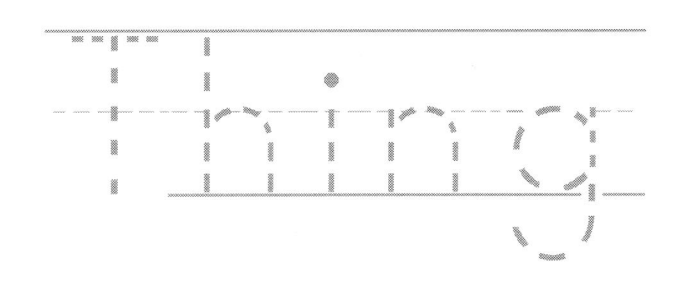

Person

Animal

Place

Thing

Noun

Color by the code.

- person — blue
- place — orange
- thing — green
- animal — yellow

Draw a Noun

Draw a person, animal, place and thing.

Person

Animal

Place

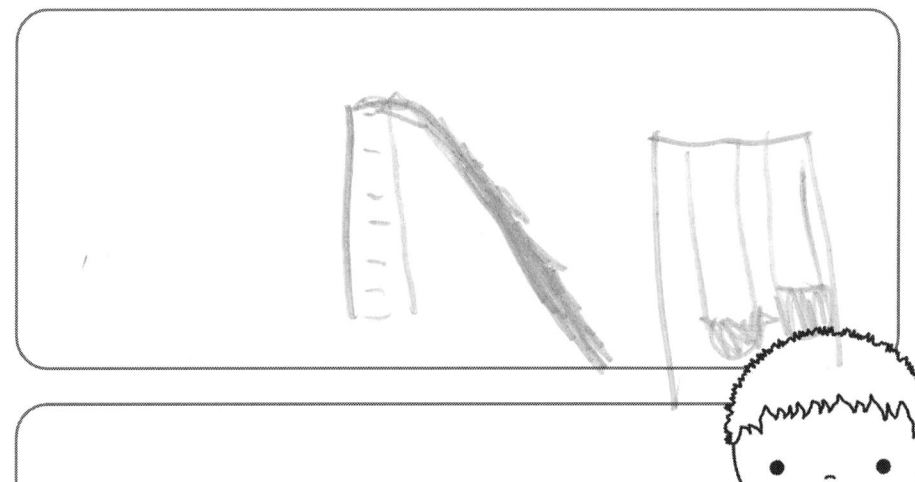

Thing

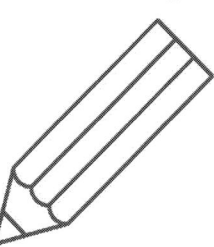

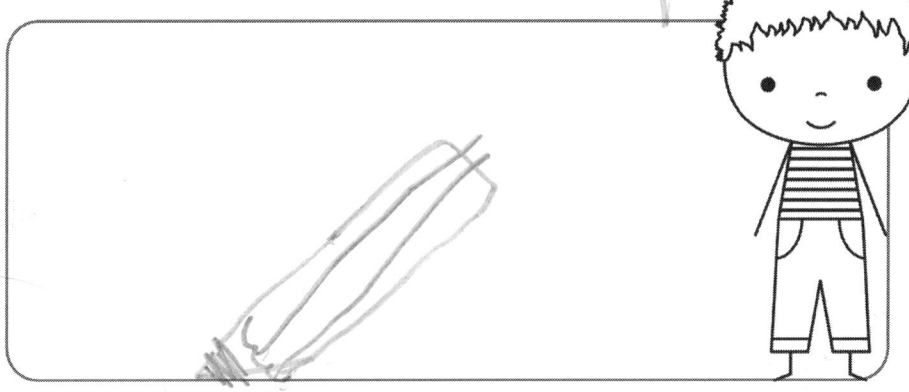

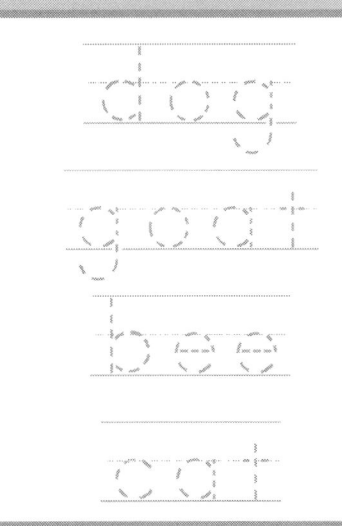

What Kind of Noun?

Read the nouns in the box. Trace the word in each box.

```
man - farm - baby - dog - hat
beach - apple - goat - milk - bee - store
teacher - mom - school - tree - cat
```

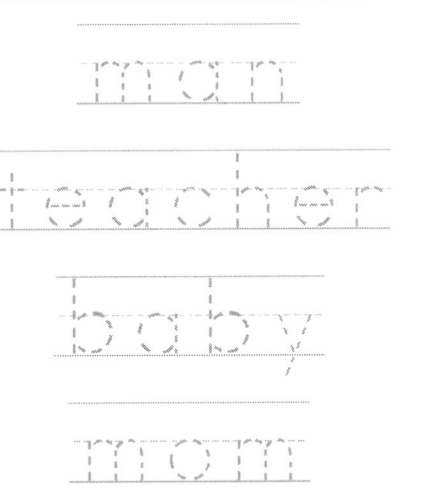

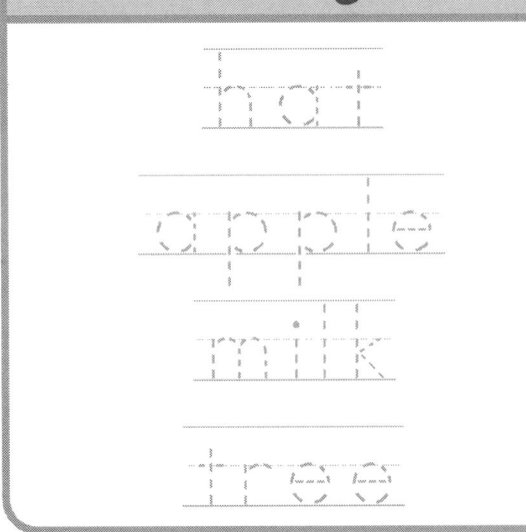

person
man
teacher
baby
mom

place
farm
beach
school
store

thing
hat
apple
milk
tree

animal
dog
goat
bee
cat

Fun Color Nouns

Color the word that matches the picture's type of noun.

(baby with bottle)	Person / Place / Animal / Thing	(apple)	Person / Place / Animal / ~~Thing~~
(grapes)	Person / Place / Animal / ~~Thing~~	(house)	Person / ~~Place~~ / Animal / Thing
(ice cream & cupcake)	Person / Place / Animal / ~~Thing~~	(airplane)	Person / Place / Animal / ~~Thing~~
(prince and princess)	~~Person~~ / Place / Animal / Thing	(kite)	Person / Place / Animal / ~~Thing~~

Noun Sort

Read the nouns in the box. Write the word in the right categories.

```
student - house - sock - duck - doctor
tiger - artist - clock - ant - mop - office
policeman - bear - school - fan - forest
```

person
1. Student Doctor Artist
2. Policeman
3. _____
4. _____

place
1. house office
2. school
3. forest
4. _____

thing
1. sock clock
2. mop fan
3. _____
4. _____

animal
1. duck ANt
2. tiger Bear
3. _____
4. _____

What Kind of Noun?

Read the nouns in the box. Trace the word in each box.

England - parent - Florida - bag - cow
monkey - Target - principal - fish - dee - aunt
jungle - fireman - paper - door - bottle

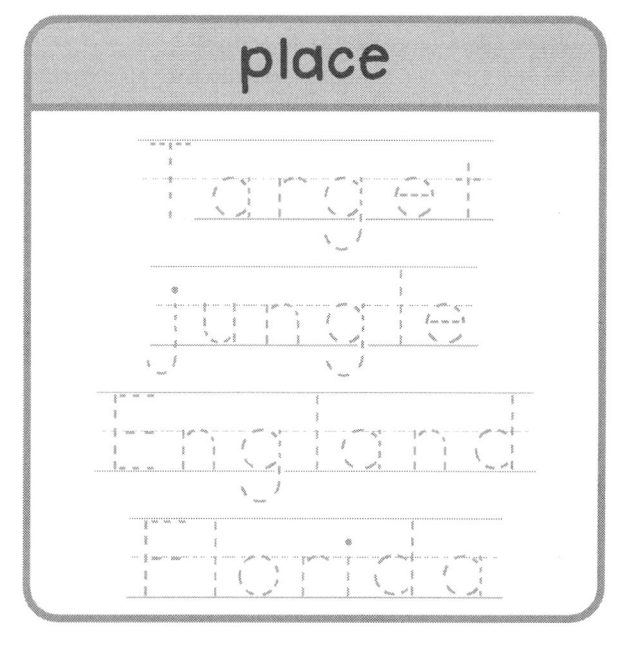

person
principal
parent
fireman
aunt

place
Target
jungle
England
Florida

thing
bag
paper
door
bottle

animal
cow
monkey
fish
deer

Noun Sort

Read the nouns in the box. Write the word into the correct box.

whale - park - zoo - uncle - hotel
book - pen - dad - mall - eraser - rice
boy - girl - frog - fox - zebra

person
1. uncle
2. dad
3. girl
4. boy

place
1. park
2. zoo
3. hotel
4. Mall

thing
1. Book
2. pen
3. eraser
4. rice

animal
1. Whale
2. frog
3. fox
4. zebra

I Can Hunt for Nouns!

Go on a hunt around your classroom or home. Write down all of the nouns that you can see!

person

Aadya

Me

Papa

Mama

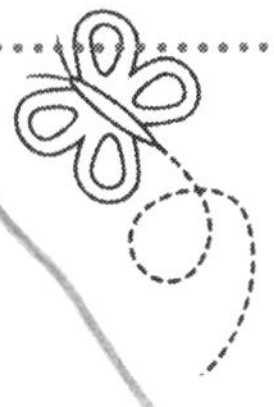

animal

place

thing

I Can Hunt for Nouns!

Go on a hunt around your classroom or home. Write down all of the nouns that you can see!

person

animal

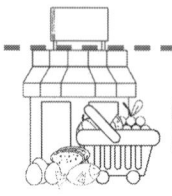

place

thing

Fun Color Nouns

Color the word that matches the picture's type of noun.

	Person / Place / Animal / Thing		Person / Place / Animal / Thing
	Person / Place / Animal / Thing		Person / Place / Animal / Thing
	Person / Place / Animal / Thing		Person / Place / Animal / Thing
	Person / Place / Animal / Thing		Person / Place / Animal / Thing

Fun Color Nouns

Color the word that matches the picture's type of noun.

	Person / Place / **Animal** / Thing		Person / Place / Animal / Thing
	Person / Place / Animal / Thing		Person / Place / Animal / Thing
	Person / Place / Animal / Thing		Person / Place / Animal / Thing
	Person / Place / Animal / Thing		Person / Place / Animal / Thing

Fun Color Nouns

Color the word that matches the picture's type of noun.

(school building)	Person / **Place** / Animal / Thing	(key)	Person / Place / Animal / **Thing**
(mouse)	Person / Place / **Animal** / Thing	(hotel with bellhop)	Person / **Place** / Animal / Thing
(pencil)	Person / Place / Animal / **Thing**	(bug)	Person / Place / **Animal** / Thing
(bird)	Person / Place / **Animal** / Thing	(boy reading at desk)	**Person** / Place / Animal / Thing

Common or Proper Nouns

A **common noun** is any person, place or thing.
A **proper noun** is a specific person, place or thing.

common nouns
- TV
- snake
- soda
- cereal
- car
- candy

proper nouns
- July
- Christmas
- USA
- Pizza Hut
- Jessie
- Elm street

July - Christmas - TV - snake
USA - Pizza Hut - soda - cereal
car - Jessie - candy - Elm Street

Common or Proper Nouns

A **common noun** is any person, place or thing.
A **proper noun** is a specific person, place or thing.

common nouns	proper nouns
- school	- Beth
school	Beth
House	NewYork
cup	MrsJones
Paper	Texas
Month	Halloween

school - Beth - New York
house - cup - Mrs.Jones - Texas
paper - Halloween - month

Proper Nouns

Think of some proper nouns for each common noun.

	Common Noun	Proper Noun
	bread	Beths Bread
	baby	moms baby
	store	Dads Store
	drug	Lilys drug
	cake	Bars cake
	bus	Lilys bus

Proper Nouns

Think of some proper nouns for each common noun.

Common Noun	Proper Noun
sock	J&J sock
home	Lilys home
yogurt	beth yogurt
girl	moms girl
flag	Eropes flag
student	mrs Lilys Good Kid

Proper Nouns

Proper nouns begin with capital letters.

Rewrite the sentence with the correct proper noun.

1. My name is (carole).

   My name is Carole.

2. I go to (grace school).

   I go to grace school

3. My best friend's name is (nathan).

   My best fiends Name is Nathan

4. We like to go to (st. patrick park)

   We like to jo st patr ick park

5. We sometimes take my dog (jacky).

   We sometimes take my dog Jacky

Plural Rules

Add -s to most nouns to make them plural

dogs

Add -es to nouns that end in -ch, -sh, -s, -x or -z

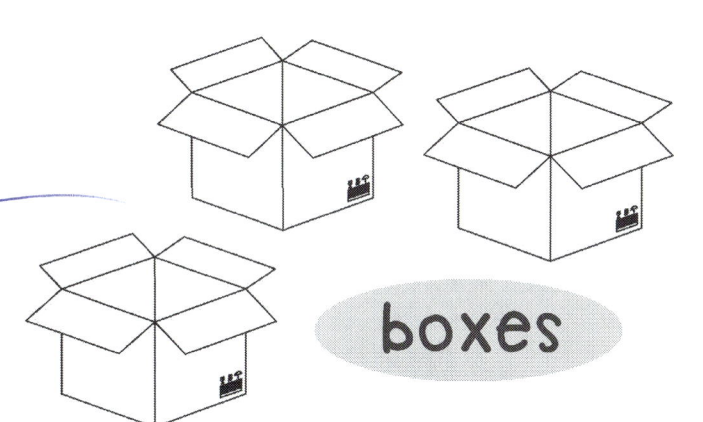

boxes

If the noun ends in -y with a consonant before the -y, change the -y to -i and add -es

cherries

If the noun ends in -f or -fe, drop the f and add -ves

leaves

Plural Nouns

- add -s
- add -es
- Drop the -y add -ies
- Irregular

Plural with -es

Add -es to nouns that end in -ch, -sh, -s, -x or -z

1. box — boxes
2. lunch — lunches
3. flash — flashes
4. mess — messes
5. fox — foxes
6. dish — dishes
7. bus — buses

Plural with -es

Add -es to nouns that end in -ch, -sh, -s, -x or -z

1. peach — peaches
2. church — Churches
3. couch — couches
4. brush — brushes
5. wish — Wishes
6. boss — bosses
7. glass — glasses

Plural with -ves ☆

Add -ves to nouns that end in -f or -fe

1. leaf — leaves
2. calf — calves
3. elf — elves
4. knife — knives
5. life — lives
6. shelf — shelves
7. giraffe — giraffes

Plural with -ves ☆

Add -ves to nouns that end in -f or -fe

1. wolf   wolves
2. thief   thieves
3. half   halves
4. shelf   shelves
5. hoof   hooves
6. wife   wlves
7. loaf   loaves

Plural with -ies

Noun ends in -y with a **consonant** before the -y, change the -y to -i and add -es

1. baby — babies
2. cherry — cherries
3. bunny — bunnies
4. spy — spies
5. puppy — puppies
6. city — cities
7. family — families

Form a Plural

Choose s or es to form a plural.

	Word	s or es
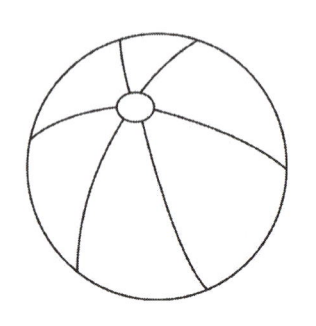	ball	balls
	fox	foxes
	key	keyes
	dish	dishs
	frog	frogs

Form a Plural

Choose s or es to form a plural.

Word	s or es
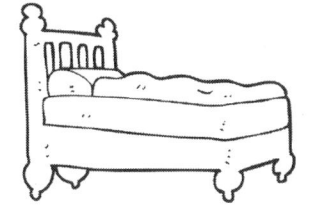 bed	beds
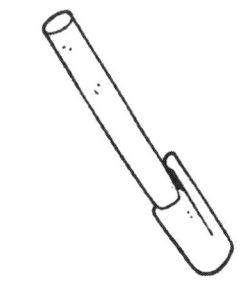 pen	pens
 house	houses
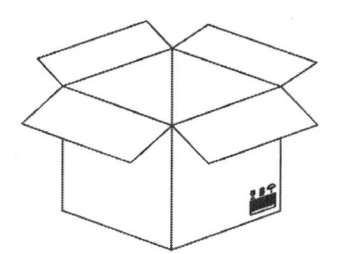 box	boxes
 bus	buses

Plural s or es

Choose s or es to form a plural.

Word	s or es
 bike	bikes
 dress	dresses
 girl	girls
 glove	gloves
 boy	boys

Plural s or es

Choose s or es to form a plural.

Word	s or es
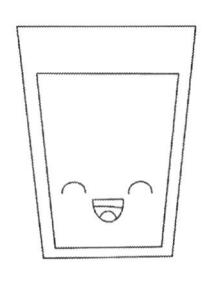 glass	glasses
 bell	bells
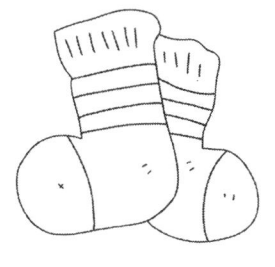 sock	sockes
 ant	antes
 wolf	wolfes

Form a Plural

Make each word plural by adding s or es at the end.

flag	flags	man	

hat		baby	

hen		sheep	

Form a Plural

Make each word plural by adding s or es at the end.

woman — women

bench — _____

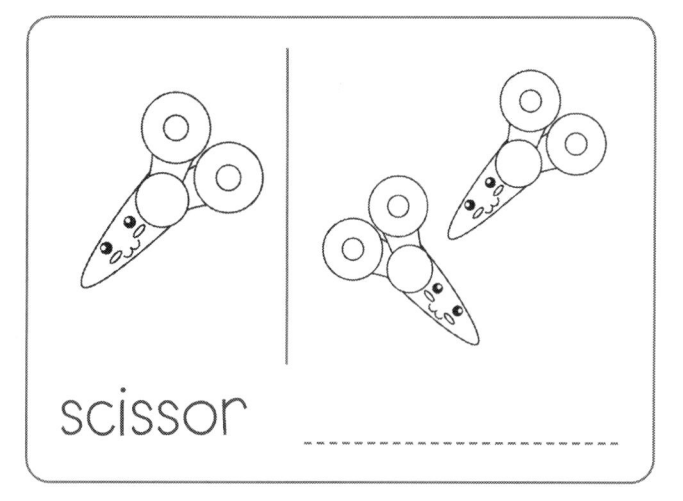

scissor — _____

bush — _____

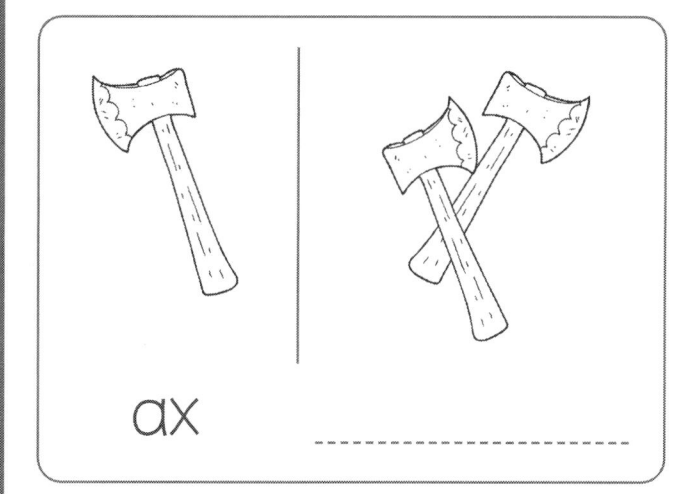

ax — _____

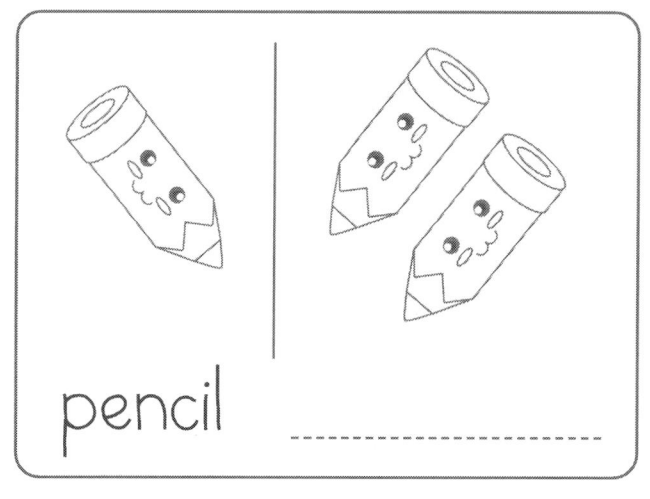

pencil — _____

Form a Plural

Make each word plural by adding s or es at the end.

leaf — *leaves*	man — *mans*
dish — *dishes*	cherry — *cherries*
ham — *hames*	bee — *bees*

Singular & Plural

Write the names in the boxes.

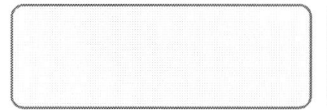

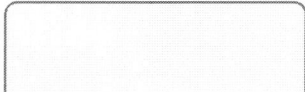

| ant | ants | | |

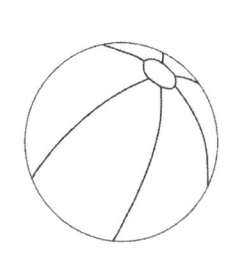

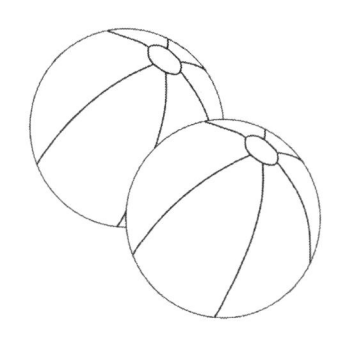

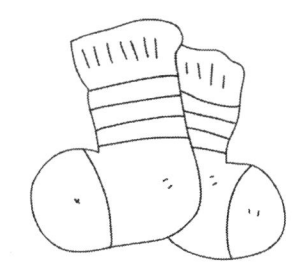

Find Plural

A noun is a word that names a person, place or thing. Plural nouns are used for more than one person, place, or thing. Circle the words that are plural.

box (boxes)	kiss kisses
bushes bush	classes class
ax axes	foxes fox
dishes dish	bench benches
zero zeroes	mix mixes

Find Plural

A noun is a word that names a person, place or thing. Plural nouns are used for more than one person, place, or thing. Circle the words that are plural.

(lamps) lamp	book books
glasses glass	ashes ash
shoe shoes	witch witches
plate plates	tree trees
dolls doll	babies baby

Find Plural

A noun is a word that names a person, place or thing. Plural nouns are used for more than one person, place, or thing. Circle the words that are plural.

| city | **(cities)** | kiss | **(kisses)** |

| **(trays)** | tray | egg | **(eggs)** |

| leaf | **(leaves)** | **(kites)** | kite |

| **(wolves)** | wolf | truck | **(trucks)** |

| **(pigs)** | pig | **(cars)** | car |

Irregular Plurals

Some plurals are irregular. They don't follow the rules, so you must remember each one. Some plural forms change in spelling.

mouse	teeth
person	children
tooth	mice
woman	people
child	women

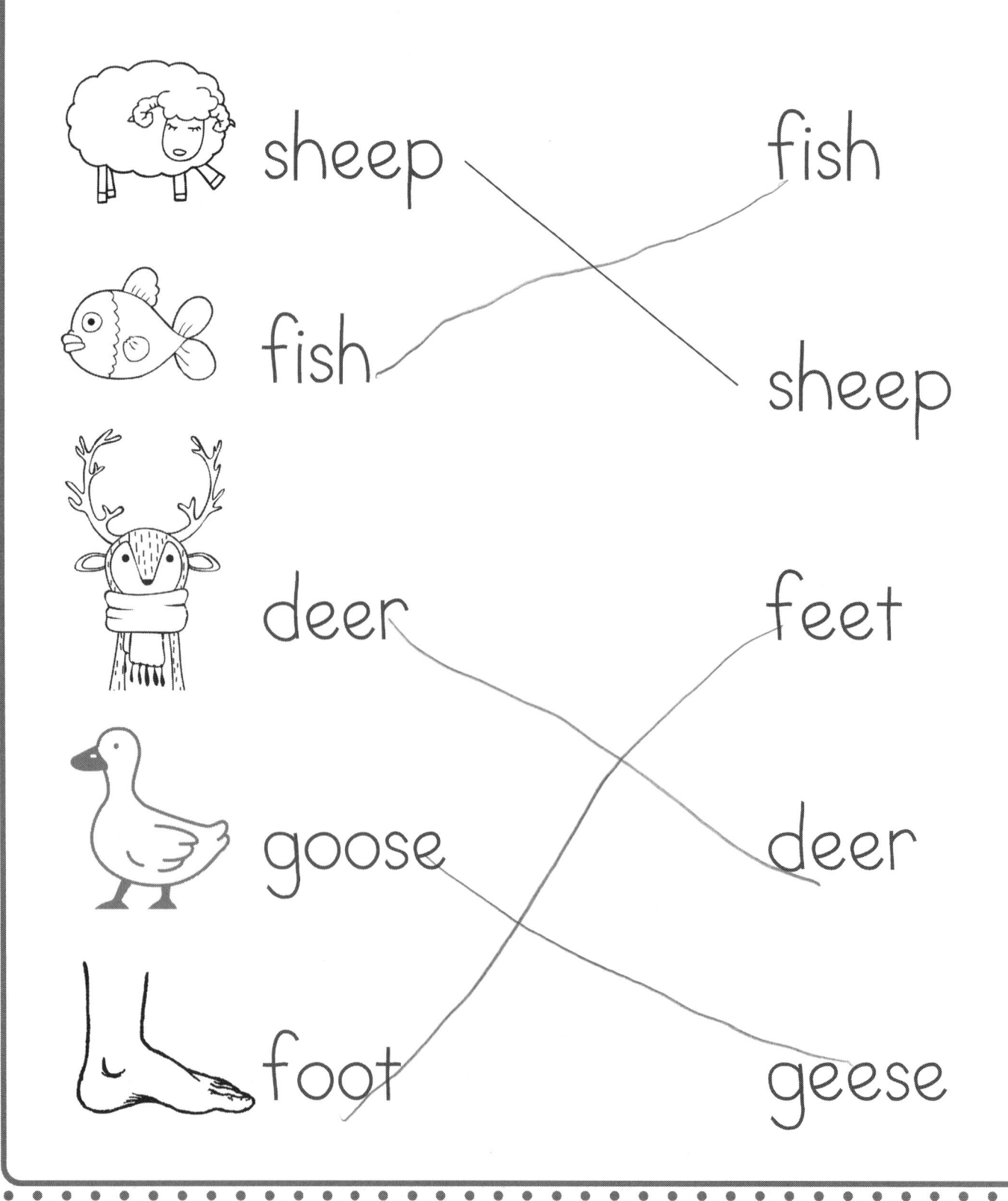

Irregular Plurals

Some plurals are irregular. They don't follow the rules, so you must remember each one. Some plural forms change in spelling.

sheep — fish
fish — sheep
deer — feet
goose — deer
foot — geese

Irregular Plurals

Some plurals are irregular. They don't follow the rules, so you must remember each one. Some plural forms change in spelling.

Singular	Plurals
cactus	cacti
wolf	wolves
man	men
wife	wives
news	news

Irregular Plurals

Some plurals are irregular. They don't follow the rules, so you must remember each one. Some plural forms change in spelling.

Singular	Plurals
leaf	leaves
quiz	quizzes
ox	oxen
policeman	policemen
tuna	tuna

Irregular Plural Nouns

Rewrite each sentence below with the correct plural noun.

geese - ~~scarves~~ - ~~men~~ - ~~children~~
~~teeth~~ - ~~mice~~ - ~~oxen~~ - ~~halves~~

1. I have ten **scarves** (scarf) in my closet.

2. Jim has two **children** (child) age two and five.

3. I brush my **theeth** (tooth) in the morning.

4. Cats like to chase **mice** (mouse).

5. There are many **oxen** (ox) on the road.

6. Two **halves** (half) make a whole.

7. Three **men** (man) entered the bank.

8. We saw a flock of **geese** (goose) in the lake.

Irregular Plural Nouns

Rewrite each sentence below with the correct plural noun.

feet - sheep - ~~people~~ - fish
thieves - loaves - hooves - lives

1. I can see __people__ (person) walking across the street.

2. Eagles fly alone, but _____(sheep) flock together.

3. The_____(thief) were caught by the police.

4. He want four_____(loaf) of bread.

5. The horse's _____(hoof) needs to be cleaned..

6. People say that a cat has nine_____(life).

7. My brother is six_____(foot) three inches tall.

8. There are always more_____(fish) in the sea.

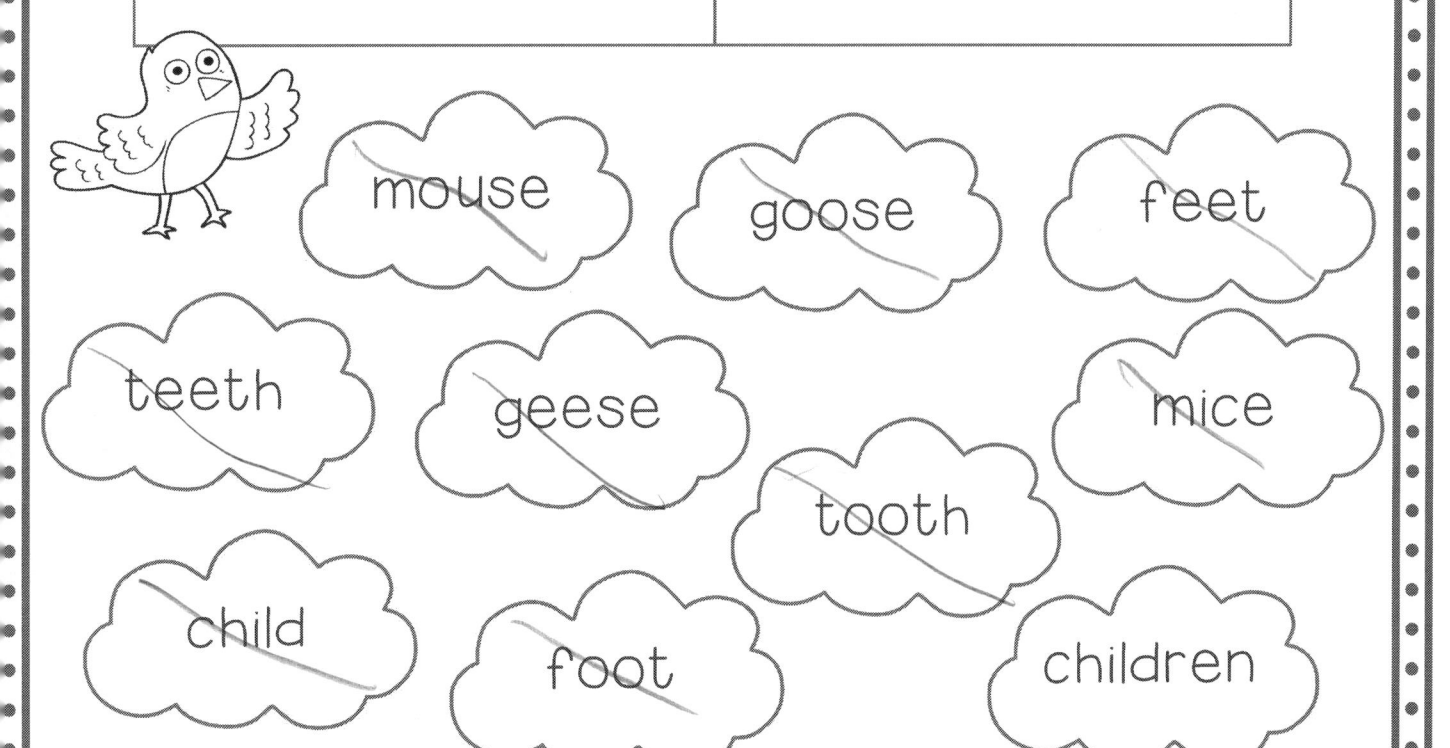

Singular or Plural

Read the words and write them in the correct column.

Singular	Plural
mouse	feet
goose	teeth
tooth	geese
child	mice
foot	children

mouse   goose   feet
teeth   geese   mice
tooth
child   foot   children

Possessive Nouns

A possessive noun shows ownership. A singular noun ends with an apostrophe and s ('s). A plural noun ends with s and an apostrophe (s'). Irregular plural nouns end with an apostrophe and s ('s).

Singular Possessive Noun	Plural Possessive Noun
teacher's lesson	teachers' lesson
class's play	classes' play
child's game	children's game

Change the noun into a possessive noun to show ownership

1. The bird <u>'s</u> nest is in my yard.

2. The squirrel <u>'s</u> tail is bushy.

3. The dog <u>'s</u> owner is very responsible.

4. The children <u>'s</u> trip to the zoo was fun.

5. The dog <u>'s</u> tail wags when he is happy.

6. The duck <u>'s</u> home is in the lake.

Possessive Nouns

Underline the correct possessive noun.
Re-write the sentence on th lines provided.

1. The (girls / <u>girl's</u>) bow was pink.

   The girl's bow was pink.

2. The (dogs / dog's) bone was big.

   _____

3. My (mom's / moms) car is red.

   _____

4. The (teacher's / teachers) shirt is big.

   _____

5. The (books / book's) pages are long.

   _____

6. The (bike's / bikes) tires are flat.

   _____

Possessive Pronouns

A possessive pronoun is a word that may take the place of a possessive noun.
Ex. his, her, hers, our, ours, your, yours their, theirs, its, my, mine.

Read each sentence. Circle the possessive pronoun.

Subject Pronouns	Possessive Pronouns
* I have a bicycle.	* The bicycle is (mine.)
* You have a bicycle.	* The bicycle is yours.
* He has a bicycle.	* The bicycle is his.
* She has a bicycle.	* The bicycle is hers.
* We have a bicycle.	* The bicycle is ours.
* They have a bicycle.	* The bicycle is theirs.

1. (Her) shoes are new.
2. There is his book.
3. His hair is dark.
4. Her hat is fancy.
5. I see their car.
6. Their lunch looks good.

Possessive Pronouns

Write the correct possessive noun in the blank.
Example. This bag's color is pink. This is Gemmy's table.

1. The __cat's__ tail is short   cat

2. The __birds__ nest is full of eggs   bird

3. The __frogs__ tongue is long.   frog

4. The __alligators__ teeth are sharp.   alligator

5. The __bunnys__ carrot is huge.   bunny

6. The __elephant's__ trunk is long.   elephant

Possessive Pronouns

Choose the best answer for each of the sentences below.

1. The dog wagges ___its___ tail to show how happy he was. (its, it's, its')

2. The book is ___Mine___ but you are welcome to read it. (mine, yours, my)

3. Please return ___my___ phone at once! (my, mine, its)

4. ___Your___ bike is so dirty!. I can't tell what color it is. (your, mine, its, my)

5. When the dog saw the skunk, it stopped in ___it's___ tracks. (it's him, its, its')

6. Your bike is a lot faster than ___my___ ✗ (my, it, mine, its)

7. Your house is much bigger than ___(ours,)___ is. (theres, ours, them, they)

Possessive Pronouns

Choose the best answer for each of the sentences below.

1. I looked everywhere for my keys but I could only find ___yours___.
   (your, yours, them)

2. I saw her dog at _____ house.
   (yourself, yours, your're)

3. I never found out _____ wallet that was. (who's, whose, who)

4. _____ dog is always so friendly.
   (there, they're, their)

5. _____ book is on my desk?
   (who's, whos, whose)

6. My sister gets along well with _____
   (you're, you, yours)

7. _____ bulling of him was not acceptable. (there, them, their)

Fun Action Verb

Fill in the blank with a verb from the word bank to complete the sentence.

> cuts - starts - finds - paints - swim
> stays - says - ~~writes~~ - digs - play

1. James __writes__ a letter to his teacher.
2. The store _____ open at night.
3. Haley _____ goodbye to her uncle.
4. Kara _____ the blue paper.
5. The boy _____ his red pen.
6. Our party _____ very soon!
7. Kara and Haley _____ a game.
8. Lily _____ a picture of a parade.
9. The animal _____ in the garden.
10. Many fish _____ in that lake.

Subject-Verb Agreement

A verb should go with the naming part of the sentence.

When the naming part of a sentence tells about one.

My <u>friend</u> write<u>s</u> letter to me.

When the naming part of a sentence tells about one.

My <u>friends</u> write letter to me.

Direction: Circle the correct verb that matches the naming part of the sentence..

1. My watch (make, (makes)) a funny noise.
2. The tree's bark (feel, feels) bumpy.
3. The fan (make, makes) the room cold.
4. Kara's dad (work, works) at home.
5. Squirrels and birds (live, lives) in that tree.
6. The fan (make, makes) the room cold.

Subject-Verb Agreement

Choose the best answer for each of the sentences below.

1. Plants __grow__ in the sun. (grow, grows)

2. The wagon _____ my brother and me. (holds, hold)

3. Mr. Joe _____ us for our help. (thank, thanks)

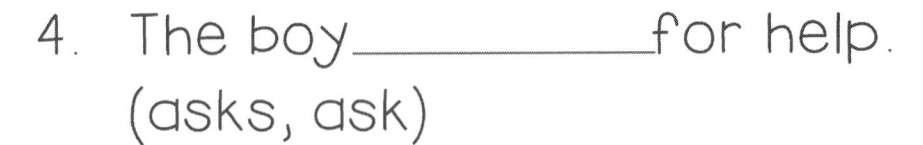

4. The boy _____ for help. (asks, ask)

5. Cats _____ all day long. (sleep, sleeps)

6. These old TVs and radios _____ great! (work, works)

7. My old sister _____ pots. (paint, paints)

Subject-Verb Agreement

Choose the best answer for each of the sentences below.

8. The girls __waters__ the grass. (water, waters)

9. The cat and the dog _____ with the toys. (play, plays)

10. The people _____ happy songs. (sing, sings)

11. Our pet bird _____ "hello". (say, says)

12. The children _____ apples and oranges. (loves, love)

13. Laura's puppy _____ the bone every time. (finds, find)

14. Pigs _____ just about any food! (eats, eat)

Subject-Verb Agreement
Do or Does

A verb should go with the naming part of the sentence.

I	YOU	HE	SHE	IT	WE	THEY
do		does			do	

Direction: Fill in the blanks with the correct verb (do, does).

1. He __does__ not want to ride a bike.

2. Why _____ they always go there?

3. James _____ not like to each tomato.

4. _____ it show any symptoms?

5. Nathan and I _____ not like carrots.

6. _____ Jenny cook with her mom?

7. _____ they swim very fast?

8. _____ we get the help from them?

9. _____ he play football?

10. _____ you want to change the pen?

Verb Tense

Verbs show an action or a state of being. The verb tense places the verb in time. The three major tense verbs can show are past, present, and future.

Sometimes it helps kids to think of the past as "yesterday," the present as "today," and the future as "tomorrow."

Past	Present	Future
I rode my bike.	I ride my bike.	I will ride my bike.
I was riding my bike.	I am riding my bike.	I will be riding my bike.
I had been riding my bike.	I have been riding my bike.	I am going to ride my bike.

Past Tense Verbs

Rule 1. To make most verbs past tense, **add -ed** to the ending
Ex. call --> call<u>ed</u>   talk --> talk<u>ed</u>

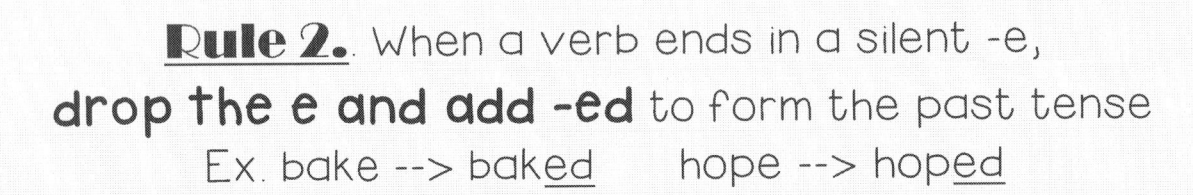

Rule 2. When a verb ends in a silent -e, **drop the e and add -ed** to form the past tense
Ex. bake --> bak<u>ed</u>   hope --> hop<u>ed</u>

Rule 3. When a verb ends in a consonant and y, **change the y to I and add -ed**
Ex. carry --> carr<u>ied</u>   copy --> cop<u>ied</u>

Write the correct past tense verbs.

1. watch   watched
2. hope   _____
3. want   _____
4. wash   _____
5. arrive _____

6. play   _____
7. enjoy _____
8. smile _____
9. visit   _____
10. work _____

Past Tense Verbs

When an action is in the past, the verb needs to be in the past tense. Often, we add -ed at the end of the verb to indicate a past action.
(or just -d if the verb ends with "e"

Direction: Draw lines to match up the present tense and past tense verbs.

pull •	• spelled	say •	• played
listen •	• waited	need •	• worked
wait •	• pulled	play •	• got
ask •	• looked	tell •	• found
look •	• ate	take •	• make
laugh •	• showed	work •	• painted
show •	• saw	make •	• said
spell •	• listened	paint •	• took
see •	• laughed	get •	• told
eat •	• asked	find •	• needed

Irregular Verbs Past Tense

An irregular verb does not follow the pattern of regular verbs in terms of adding an -ed for the past.

Present Tense	Past Tense
see	saw
eat	
drive	
ride	
draw	
dive	
hide	
run	
tell	
fall	
read	
sleep	

Irregular Verbs Past Tense

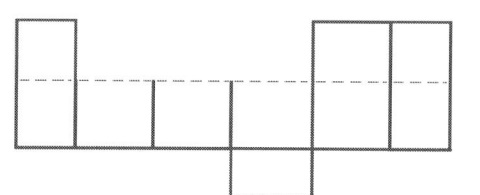

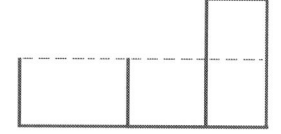

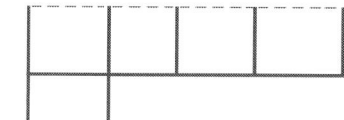

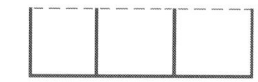

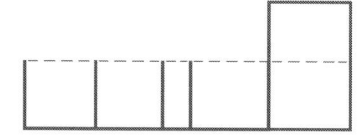

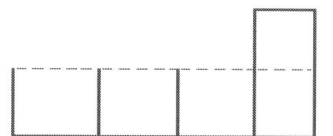

Write the past tense of each irregular verb below.

Present Tense   Past Tense

teach

meet

grow

run

cry

win

go

Irregular Verbs Past Tense

Write the past tense of each irregular verb below.

Present Tense   Past Tense

teach

meet

grow

run

cry

win

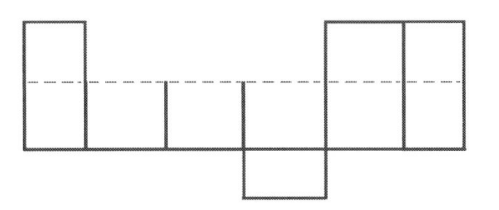

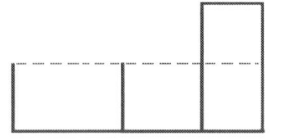

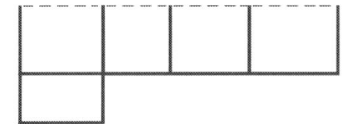

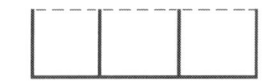

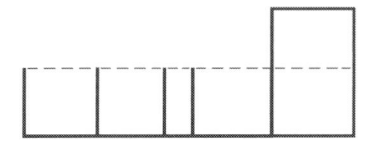

go

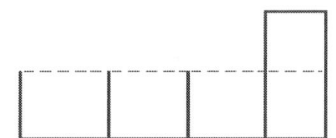

Irregular Verbs Past Tense

Rewrite each sentence below with the corect past tense verb.

1. Last week, I ___went___ (go) horseback riding.

2. Kara's mother _____ (tells) her a bedtime story.

3. The sun _____ (shines) brightly and birds were singing.

4. Nathan _____ (draws) a picture of his family.

5. _____ (Do) you wash the dishes like I asked you to?

6. My car _____ (breaks) down on the way to work.

7. Jenny _____ (wears) a beautiful dress to the party.

8. Tony _____ (eats) nothing but ham sandwiches.

9. Mrs. Erica _____ (teaches) her granddaughter how to sew.

Inflectional Endings -ed and -ing

A word ending is something that you add to the end of a word. The endings -ed and -ing can tell you more about the action part of a sentence.

The -ing ending tells you that something is still happening. The -ed ending tells you that something has finished.

Read each action word. Write the new endings for each word.

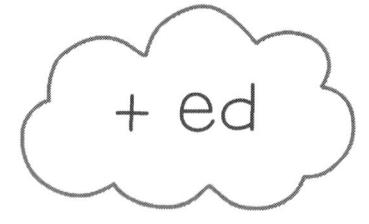

Verb (action verb)	+ ing	+ ed
1. walk	walking	walked
2. spill		
3. help		
4. look		
5. plant		
6. jump		

Present, Past, and Future

Draw a circle around the action verb in each sentence. On the line, tell whether the verb is past tense, present tense, or future tense.

Example:

Jimmy (played) football yesterday.   past tense

He (plays) football everyday.   present tense

We (will go to) Jimmy's baseball game.   future tense

1. Jimmy will choose a baseball bat. _____

2. He steps up to the plate. _____

3. The pitcher tossed the ball. _____

4. Jimmy will swing hard. _____

5. The ball struck the bat. _____

6. The ball flied through the air. _____

7. It landed over the fence. _____

8. Jimmy will run around the bases. _____

9. The crowd screams loudly. _____

10. He will slide into home plate. _____

To be: Present Tense
am / is / are

Use **is** if the sentence is about **one** person, animal, place, or thing.

Ex. **Mary** is funny.   **It** is soft.

Use **are** if the sentence is about **more than one** person, animal, place, or thing. Also use **are** if the sentence is about **you**.

Ex. **Jake and Ron** are late.   **We** are behind you.

Use **am** if the sentence is about **I**.

Ex. **I** am here.

Complete each sentence with the word am, is or are.

1. The books_____ new.

2. There_____ hot coffee in the cup.

3. I_____ writing a story at my desk.

4. The bread and knife_____ on the table.

5. The bottle_____ full of milk.

To be: Present Tense

Choose "is", "am", or "are" to complete the sentences.

is / am / are

1. Jenny _____ swimming in the pool.

2. The school bell _____ ringing.

3. I _____ Marcus.

4. Ships _____ sailing in the sea.

5. I _____ not a rabbit.

6. Birds _____ flying in the sky.

7. We _____ happy.

8. Marcus and Jenny _____ friends.

9. These children _____ playing in the park.

10. The tiger _____ feeling hungry.

11. I _____ not a student.

12. This _____ a lotus flower.

To be: Past Tense was / were

Use **was** if the sentence is about **one** person, animal, place, or thing.

Ex. **Mary** was funny.   **It** was soft.

Use **were** if the sentence is about **more than one** person, animal, place, or thing. Also use **were** if the sentence is about **you**.

Ex. **Jake and Ron** were late.   **You** were so nice.

Complete each sentence with the word was or were.

1. The boys_____climbing on the tree.

2. She_____shopping with her mother.

3. I_____so happy yesterday.

4. My dog_____chasing her cat.

5. Where_____they playing.

6. You_____busy on Monday.

7. We_____at school last Sunday.

Verb to be

Use the correct form : Complete each setence with the word is, am, are, was or were.

is / am / are / was / were

1. You_____funny in that show. (was, were)

2. The back door_____open. (is, are)

3. I_____six years old today! (am, are)

4. Bob's dog_____on his bed. (were, was).

5. The day_____sunny. (was, were)

6. The girls_____all in class. (was, were)

7. My sisters_____at school today. (are, am)

8. The oranges_____in the basket. (am, are)

9. The men_____outside in the rain. (am, are)

10. You_____away a long time! (were, was)

11. Jen's uncle_____glad to see her. (is, are)

12. My rabbit_____white and brown. (is, are)

Verb to have
has / have

Use **has** if the sentence is about **one** person, animal, place, or thing.

Ex. **Pat** has a pen.   **He** has two balloons.

Use **have** if the sentence is about **more than one** person, animal, place, or thing. Also use **have** if the sentence is about **you** or **I**.

Ex. **The boys** have many friends.
You have a nice bag.   **I** have a cat.

Complete each sentence with the word has or have.

1. The painters_____red and yellow paint.

2. Ducks_____flat feet.

3. This zoo_____ten monkeys!

4. Those horses_____long brown tails.

5. I_____lunch with my friends everyday.

6. The men _____black coats and hats.

Articles
A and An are called articles

Use **a** before a word that starts with a **consonant sound.**

Ex. Pat has **a** pen.   I ate **a** banana.

Use **an** before a word that starts with a **vowel sound.**

Ex. **An** ant walked up the tree.

Fill in the blanks with the correct articles "a" or "an".

_____ ant

_____ ring

_____ cow

_____ apple

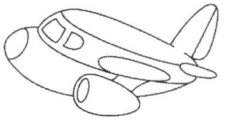

_____ airplane

_____ key

Articles

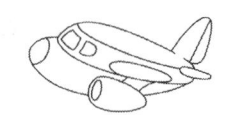

Complete each setence with article a or an.

a / an

1. Jen has_____aunt who is a teacher.

2. There's_____fly in my lunch!

3. _____king has many people to help him.

4. Living on_____farm can be hard work.

5. _____owl flew out of the tree.

6. Mrs. Smile has_____truck.

7. I put some cookies on _____dish.

8. I have _____uncle who lives near you.

9. I put my puppy in_____wagon.

10. I have_____idea for my new story.

11. We played _____easy game in class.

12. Did you buy_____new car?

Adjective

An **adjective** is a word that tells about a person, animal, place, or thing.

Some adjectives tell how a noun **looks**, **sounds**, **tastes**, **smells**, or **feels**.

Ex. The sun looks **bright**.
The drums sound **loud**.
These cookies taste **sweet**.
The air smells **fresh**.
My hair feels **soft**.

Circle the correct adjective in each sentence.

1. Ants are (big / small)

2. Ants have (short / long) legs.

3. Ants are (light / heavy).

4. Ants are (strong / weak).

5. Ants have (small / big) body.

Adjective

Complete each setence with correct adjective.

1. The drum makes a _____ noise. (sound, loud).

2. The ground is _____ there. (flat, village)

3. Joe drinks a _____ cup of milk. (food, full)

4. Jane lives in a _____ house. (door, blue).

5. This bed is too _____. (hard, hand)

6. The baby's hands are _____. (pocket, dirty)

7. A _____ bat flew by. (black, bird)

8. His teacher is _____. (tall, leg)

9. The rug feels _____. (soft, sleep)

10. I can carry this _____ bag. (fast, light)

11. We swim on _____ days. (yummy, hot)

12. The TV is too _____! (lound, tasty)

13. I love picnics on _____ days. (sunny, dirty)

Comparative

Some adjectives compare people, animals, places, or things.

Comparative adjectives compare two people, animals, places, or things. They end in **-er**.
Ex. He is **taller** than his sister.

Superlative adjectives compare more than two people, animals, places, or things. They end in **-est**.
Ex. He is **tallest** person in his class.

Write the correct form of comparative and superative.

1. Your cake is _____ than Wendy's. (sweet)

2. Your shoes are _____ than mine. (wet)

3. Today is the _____ day so far! (hot)

4. Joe is the _____ man in Kingwood. (tall)

5. This is the _____ hill in Lowell. (high).

Adjective

Comparative adjectives   than --> er to the adj.
Superative adjectives   the --> est to the adj.

Practice: Comparative and superative.

1. Mr. Hill is_____than Mrs. Hill (old).

2. Canada is_____than Mexico. (cold)

3. This is the_____night of the year. (long)

4. The Brown's cat is_____than ours. (fat).

5. My mom's bed is_____than my bed. (soft)

6. My eyes are_____than yoursl. (dark)

7. Snowy is the_____goat of all. (white)

8. An ant is_____than a bee. (light)

9. My boat is_____than Susan's. (new)

10. That's the_____story in the book. (short)

Prepositions

Some words tell where something is or where something happens.

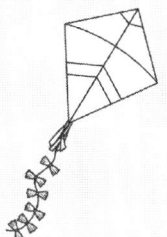

Ex. The cat is under the bed.
She jumps on the bed.

A few examples are **above, behind, beside, between, by, in, in front of, inside, next to, on, outside,** and **under**.

Read each sentence and circle the preposition.

The cookies are in front of the cupcake.

The cat is under the umbrella.

He is sitting on the bench.

She is under the table.

Prepositions

behind - next to - in front of - in - beside
above - outside - between - by - on

Choose and write the word to complete the sentence.

1. I run_____the other people.

2. The dog's food is_____her water.

3. My father wears a brown cap_____his head.

4. Rabbits dig_____the ground.

5. A bat is flying right_____your head!

6. Sometimes my cat sleeps_____my dog.

7. The live_____the town.

8. Joe walks his dog_____Joe walks his dog.

9. The bird flew_____two tall trees.

10. A tree fell right_____me!

Conjunctions

Conjunctions (like and, but, or, and so) are used to put words and sentences together.

AND: Use and to show that things go together.
   Ex. Greg and Kate are playing a game.

BUT: Use but to show that things are different or opposite.   Ex. I want to read, but my sister wants to play with me.

OR: Use or to show a choice.
   Ex. Do you want to go to the zoo or the park?

SO: Use so to show that something happens because of something else.
Ex. Today is my birthday, so my mom baked a cake.

and

or

so

but

Conjunctions

and / or / but / so

Complete the sentence with the correct conjunction.

1. I Jen draws_____sings at the same time.

2. The ball is not in the wagon_____the pool.

3. Joe_____Jane play in the same park.

4. Did you walk alone_____with a friend?

5. Is your teacher Mr.White_____Mr.Ruth?

6. The dish was dirty,_____dad washed it.

7. The baby walks,_____he does not talk.

8. Mike_____Min play side by side.

9. Ken was not home,_____I called Mike.

10. Joy missed the bus,_____she had to walk.

Conjunctions

and / or / but / so

Complete the sentence with the correct conjunction.

1. Mom was tired,_____she went to bed.

2. School is closed,_____the zoo is open..

3. Jame has a balloon,_____it poped.

4. Lily_____I miss you so much!

5. Do you want cake_____a cookie?

6. The parade is starting,_____let's go now!

7. Kara has a bike,_____she never rides it..

8. We are getting a puppy_____a kitten!

9. I like apples,_____I does not like oranges.

10. It is dark outside,_____it is cold, too.

Contraction

A contraction is a short form of two words. The words are put together, and some letters are left out. An apostrophe (') shows where the letters are left out.

is not --> isn't

he is --> he's

The contraction can't is special. It is short for cannot. To make the contraction, drop the letters n and o, and put an apostrophe in their place.

cannot --> can't

The contraction won't is also special. It is short for will not. The spelling changes when the two words are put together.

will not --> won't

Contraction

Read the contractions below. Write the correct contraction to finish the sentence.

| didn't | it's | isn't | don't | can't |
| she's | we're | I'll | he'll | does't |

1. Mike _____ eat all of his lunch. (did not)

2. A flying squirrel _____ really fly. (does not)

3. It _____ too cold outside. (is not)

4. _____ going to the circus! (we are)

5. _____ time for dinner! (It is)

6. _____ really going to miss this house! (She is)

7. The baby birds _____ fly yet. (cannot)

8. Grandpa said _____ miss me. (he will)

9. Mr. and Mrs. B _____ have any pets. (do not)

10. _____ hold your books for you. (I will)

Contraction

Read the contractions below. Write the correct contraction to finish the sentence.

| weren't | can't | I'm | you'll | haven't |
| isn't | we're | we're | aren't | it'll |

1. When we go to Texas, _____ be hot. (it will)

2. The goats _____ in the barn. (were not.)

3. Joe and John _____ here yet. (are not)

4. Pete _____ come to my party today. (cannot)

5. _____ nine years old. (I am)

6. _____ ready for our trip. (we are)

7. _____ never guess what I saw today! (you will)

8. We _____ done to J's house before. (have not)

9. That book _____ mine. (is not)

10. _____ hold your books for you. (I will)

Capitalization

Capitalize the names of people and pets.
My sister is named <u>Laura</u>.
Her dog is named <u>Buddy</u>.

Rewrite each sentence with correct capitalization.

1. The squirrel ran away from jim.

   _____

2. The boys ride bikes with mike.

   _____

3. Today jimmy made a bed for his kitten, ted.

   _____

4. jenny named her new cat oscar.

   _____

5. Where is lola going with those people?

   _____

Capitalization

Capitalize the names of people and pets.
My sister is named <u>Laura</u>.
Her dog is named <u>Buddy</u>.

Rewrite each sentence with correct capitalization.

1. I love rex. He is my dog.

   _____

2. Last night bill was sad.

   _____

3. Yes, jenny is my little Sister.

   _____

4. Please bring me my Shoes, jon.

   _____

5. Their Horse gus runs fast!

   _____

Capitalization

Capitalize the names of months and days of the week.

We go away on Friday.

We are gone for all of March.

Rewrite each sentence with correct capitalization.

1. Dad worked hard last may.

   _____

2. I like the warm mornings in july.

   _____

3. There is no school on monday.

   _____

4. I don't want to work on saturday!.

   _____

5. They picked apples on Friday, september 5.

   _____

Capitalization

Capitalize the names of months and days of the week.

We go away on <u>Friday</u>.
We are gone for all of <u>March</u>.

Rewrite each sentence with correct capitalization.

1. We walked to the park on saturday.

   _____

2. What time on saturday should I come over?

   _____

3. He took two trips in november.

   _____

4. My Birthday is march 12. When is yours?

   _____

5. On monday we ate a big Lunch.

   _____

Capitalization

Capitalize the first word of a sentence
<u>That</u> dress is nice.

Capitalize I
Jan and <u>I</u> sing.

Rewrite each sentence with correct capitalization.

1. The girls and i run around outside.

   _____

2. after i eat, I have to help my mom.

   _____

3. Where are you going? May i go, too?.

   _____

4. my dog ran off, so i went after her.

   _____

5. look out! that paint is wet!

   _____

Capitalization

Capitalize the first word of a sentence
<u>That</u> dress is nice.

Capitalize I
Jan and <u>I</u> sing.

Rewrite each sentence with correct capitalization.

1. he wrote me a letter.

   _____

2. stay away from the fire. It's hot!

   _____

3. we saw a pony on the farm.

   _____

4. cows live on farms. They make milk.

   _____

5. no, the teacher isn't here now.

   _____

Made in the USA
Columbia, SC
20 November 2023